THE BEAUTIFUL
ANIMALS OF KENYA

MOHAMED AMIN
DUNCAN WILLETTS
BRIAN TETLEY

Text Book Centre

This edition published 1993 by
Text Book Centre Ltd.
Kijabe Street,
P.O. Box 47540
Nairobi
Kenya

First published 1989

Second Impression 1993

© Camerapix 1989

ISBN 1 874041 26 1

This book was designed and produced by
Camerapix Publishers International
P. O. Box 45048, Nairobi, Kenya

Editor: John Karmali
Design: Craig Dodd
Typeset: Nazma Rawji

Half-title: King of Beasts, the African lion. Title page: African elephant.
Contents page: Zebra at sundown. Page 6: Female lesser kudu.
Page 7: Giraffe, tallest animal in the world. Page 8: Cheetah, fastest animal in the world.

Printed in Hong Kong by South China Printing Co.

Contents

Introduction

Kenya covers more than half a million square kilometres with almost every form of environment known to man and animal, from permanent snow to true desert. Mountain massifs, running from north to south like a backbone, lie along its centre, bisecting the Equator. On either side, from east to west, a series of plateaux step upward like stairways – from the humid, monsoon-blown palm belt of the coast, through the savannah hinterland, over the highlands and down again, through tea and coffee plantations, to the western sugar belt and the bowl of Lake Victoria.

Throughout this land, in whichever direction you go, can be found one of the greatest displays of wildlife in the world; some truly unique, much of it rare, and a few whose lineage goes back long before the first ancestors of mankind evolved on the shores of Lake Turkana, a remote and distant inland sea in Kenya's far north. A large area on its eastern shores forms one of more than sixty nature sanctuaries established to preserve for future generations a wildlife, marine, and prehistoric heritage which has few equals. Indeed, combined with the wildlife resources of Kenya's sister states, Tanzania and Uganda, nothing like it can be found anywhere else.

The diversity of environment has encouraged and now preserves these creatures bright and beautiful, great and small, wild and wonderful, allowing them to roam freely within their natural habitat. Some are specific to the highland plateaux and the forested and moorland mountain slopes; others roam between this environment and the plains and savannah.

Some exist in pockets, around lakes and in swamps, while others live only in isolated and carefully conserved groups. A few are under threat from ruthless and well-organized

poachers. And, for some, protection has proved benevolent and encouraged them to wax abundant. Few or many, they make up the *Beautiful Animals of Kenya*, which yearly draw more and more visitors to the country.

Kenya's first national park, Nairobi, opened its gates in 1946. By Independence in 1963 there was a network of twelve parks and reserves. Expansion was swift. Within the next twenty-five years they grew to more than sixty. They range from the combined area of the twin Tsavo parks, which cover more than 20,000 square kilometres, to the tiny postage stamp-sized Saiwa National Park which covers under three square kilometres. In several of these sanctuaries, luxury lodges and permanent camps provide an ideal background from which to observe and delight in the remarkable spectrum of wildlife which abounds in Kenya, some of it extremely specialized in its mode, and range, of living.

There are more than eighty major species – from the 'Big Five', the most cherished trophies of all among the old hunting fraternity, to tiny antelope like the dik-dik which is no bigger than a rabbit.

Compare it with the majesty of a full-grown eland, the largest member of the same family, and you will need no more convincing of the remarkable versatility and variety of Africa's fauna.

Here you can watch the stealthy stalk of the three great predators – lion, leopard, and cheetah – and the startled zig-zag flight of impala or Thomson's gazelle as they try to elude an inevitable destiny.

With luck, you may see a smaller, more timid predator: an appealing and baby-faced killer that pounces on insects and small rodents, the bat-eared fox.

Somewhere, around the water's edge for certain, you'll hear the haunting call of one of Africa's great raptors, the fish eagle.

Here in the Kenya wilderness, in mountain forest or sun-scorched savannah grasslands, nature's grand, primaeval drama is re-enacted daily as it may well have been from the dawn of time. Death is the constant companion.

With stately, majestic gait the elephant, the world's largest land creature, plods along the time-worn trails carved through these wildernesses by the passages of the herds.

Tick birds perch on their massive shoulders, as they do on the buffalo and rhinoceros, cleaning their skins of parasites. Somewhere in the shade of a tree a pride of lion slumber.

Scampering through the long grass, nervous of every shadow and rustle of wind, moves one of the shy and tiny denizens of this world; perhaps a dik-dik, maybe a hedgehog or squirrel.

Each of these creatures, the hunters and the hunted, the scavenger and the parasite, has a role to play in this great daily pageant of life and death at which you are a privileged observer.

This book is designed to help the visitor and the enthusiast find where to see The *Beautiful Animals of Kenya* and get to know them better.

Opposite: Lioness on kill. Females kill more frequently than males.

Below: Lion at water.

Opposite: Lioness with cubs: when lion take over a pride they generally kill any offpsring not their own.

1. Cats, Great and Small

For most visitors to Kenya's game sanctuaries the implicit savagery of nature's eternal kill-or-be-killed ritual is found only in films and television or the pages of books and magazines. Yet, kill the hunters do – and frequently. The size of the kill, of course, varies according to the size of the species.

The **Lion**, unmistakable in size and majesty, is the largest of Kenya's three big cats. It weighs up to 280 kilos. Its amber-coloured eyes, like those of the leopard, differ from those of most cats. They are circular, not oval. Although basically lazy, the lion is extremely powerful – able, at one leap, to clear a barrier almost four metres high or a chasm as wide as twelve metres. Resourceful killers, lion hunt communally. The kill is swift. In a short burst, lion can run down their preferred prey – zebra, hartebeest, wildebeest, and other gazelles – at a top speed of around sixty-four kilometres an hour. The favourite method is a pounce on the victim's back, dragging it to the ground and seizing it by the throat. Another method is suffocation by holding the victim's muzzle in its mouth.

Lion normally kill more than they can eat, but will eat carrion left by other predators. In an ordinary year, on average, a lion or lioness accounts for nineteen head of game at a weight of about 114 kilos for each kill. They wolf down as much as twenty-five kilos of flesh in one meal. Thereafter, they may go without eating for three to five days. Lioness kill more frequently than lion but the male is always the first to eat, the females second and the young last of all. In times of scarcity, cubs receive a cuff around the ear and threats to warn them off. Many die of starvation and vitamin deficiency, a natural method of population control. Lion prides often total as many as thirty animals, mostly females and young. Territorial creatures, they mark their range – up to 160 square kilometres – by urination. The familiar roar, rarely heard during daytime, carries as far as eight kilometres and signals territorial ownership. This ability to roar – caused by a peculiar arrangement of the vocal mechanism – is shared by the leopard, tiger and jaguar. So powerful is this roar it stirs the dust two metres away.

Lion are phenomenal lovers. There is no mating season and lioness come into heat at least once a month. Though the female feigns aggression during the initial approaches, just as the lion feigns indifference afterwards, it is clearly responsive. The act, though brief – it rarely lasts longer than six seconds – is frequent, as often as thirty to forty times a day. In one instance, mating lion and lioness were observed to couple 360 times in one week.

Lion are found almost everywhere in Kenya. There are a number of prides in Nairobi National Park about eight kilometres from the city centre. Occasionally, they break out of the park bounds and head into the nearby Karen and Langata suburbs or the industrial area. One held watchmen at bay at the General Motors assembly plant in the early 1980s, and in the 1970s several valuable horses in Karen and Langata were killed by a renegade escapee.

For many people the **Leopard** is the most beautiful of Kenya's cats. Much smaller than the lion, it weighs an average of thirty to eighty-two kilos. Its sandy fur is covered with exquisite dark rosettes.

Leopard move mainly at night. Only rarely are they seen

Above: Lioness and cub.

Opposite: Mating lion and lioness rarely rest – coupling as often as 360 times in a single week.

Right: Lion spend much of the day lazing in the shade.

during the day, resting up in the branches of a shady tree. Superb hunters, they prefer to kill without stalking – by leaping from the branches of a tree and seizing its neck or throat. Leopard kills last longer than those of the lion. What they cannot eat immediately, they haul up a tree, out of reach of scavengers. In this way they monopolize it – even if towards the end it become rancid. Leopard kill anything from small rodents to medium to large gazelle and antelope. They even eat fish and come readily to carrion.

They are usually solitary, but during mating, and when the female is pregnant, move about in pairs. There are an average of two to three cubs a litter. Leopard have the same vocal mechanism as the lion. Their roar, a grunting cough, sounds like a saw cutting rough wood.

Hunted ruthlessly for their skin, their elusive habits and solitude have helped to save them. Leopard live around (and sometimes in) urban settlements and are only noticed when pets and livestock begin to disappear. For all that, they are often beneficial, feeding on animals harmful to crops.

In the 1980s one was found in the yard of a house in Ngara, Nairobi, no more than five minutes walk from the city centre. Leopard still live in City Park, a forest preserve in the Parklands suburb of Nairobi not far from Ngara. Leopard are scattered throughout Kenya and range from sea level up to around 4,000 metres high on the Aberdare range and Mount Kenya. One place where there is a reasonable chance of observing them, even during daytime, is in the Maasai Mara.

Although seen more frequently than the leopard, the **Cheetah** in fact is a more specialized animal. Most slender of the three big cats – with an average weight of between forty-three to sixty-three kilos – its oval eyes and gentle demeanour make it the most appealing.

Evolution has given cheetahs – deep chest, slender body, long thin legs – all the attributes they need for speed. Indeed, nothing in nature equals their swiftness on land. The fastest animal in the world, it has recorded a speed of more than 112 kilometres an hour. But the burst is brief, and always leaves the cheetah gasping for breath. Sometimes cheetah are so short of air their victims escape the capture hold – a slashing, claw-raking blow to the flank – and make off. At other times, a more dominant killer or scavenger – lion or hyaena – will move in and steal the kill from the panting cheetah.

Cheetah live and hunt alone or in pairs; at most in groups of six. Cubs are usually born in litters of two to four, sometimes more. The purr of the mother, like an overloud dynamo, trembles in the still air as she grooms her helpless, grey-coloured young. The characteristic black spots develop some months later at about the time the young start to roam on their own, only to be recalled by the mother's chirruping cry.

Cheetah occupy relatively open areas where they hunt by sight, catch by speed and kill with a throat hold. Although much rarer than the leopard, these superb specialists of the cat species are almost certain to be seen in the Nairobi, Amboseli, Tsavo, Samburu, Meru, and Mara sanctuaries.

Of Kenya's other cats, the **Serval**, with its long legs and large oval ears, is distinguished by its medium build. It weighs

around thirteen to fifteen kilos. The serval's main food is rodents but ranging far and wide across Kenya – from lowland savannah to high mountain moorland – this adaptable cat also eats lizards, fish, vegetables, birds, and small antelope. To catch birds it leaps high into the air as the victim takes off. Litters usually number between two and four and the call of the kitten is a plaintive high-pitched *how . . . how . . . how*. The young are born and reared in old porcupine and antbear burrows. The serval is an agile tree climber. They make delightful pets.

Sloping through the bush at night, its large, elegant and tufted ears quivering and alert, the **Caracal** is all too rare. Its flat head, long legs, and powerful shoulders give it the proportions of a lynx. With hind legs longer than the forelegs, few cats can emulate the caracal's sudden spring into the air to pull down a bird in mid-flight, sometimes as high as three metres – for its size, a phenomenal distance.

The soft thick coat has no distinct stripes or spots. The tail is noticeably shorter than that of any other African cat. The caracal is also found in the near East, India and Arabia.

Looking just like an overgrown domestic tabby, few cat lovers can resist the appeal of the **African Wild Cat**. With less distinct markings and shorter tail, they are easy to distinguish from the home variety.

Being nocturnal, they spend the day hidden in bush, rock crevices or tall grass, emerging at night to hunt birds, rodents, snakes, lizards, hares, and young or small antelope. They also prey on domestic stock and poultry. These cats often interbreed with domestic cats.

Although they are not cats, civets, genets and mongooses, all carnivorous viverrids, are included in this chapter for convenience.

The exotic and alluring scents of the perfume makers have their origins in some strange places. It is unlikely that anybody seeing the **Civet**, a long-legged, dog-like creature, stalking through the Kenya bush would associate it with such fragrances as those of Chanel or Cardin. Yet this carnivore produces a much sought-after ingredient of the perfumer's art.

In its raw state, deposited from an anal scent gland, this secretion is a nauseating oily substance. But blended with other ingredients into a subtle mixture of fragrance, it commands high prices and the respect of users who, no doubt, would be appalled to know the exact location of its origins. As a result of this musky secretion, however, the civet has been domesticated in Ethiopia and reared to produce this commodity.

It is the largest of the viverrid family and weighs between nine to twenty kilos. The long coarse body has a varied pattern of black spots. The civet, which is found in savannah and sometimes dense forest, hides during the day in old burrows. It feeds on fruits, carrion, rodents, birds, eggs, lizards, small game, frogs, slugs, snails, and insects. It has a low-pitched cough and growl.

Another species, the **Palm (or Two-Spotted) Civet**, spends most of its life in trees or vines and mews like a cat.

The **Small-Spotted (or Neumann's) Genet** is widespread through Kenya's savannah country. It is also found in south and west Europe, the Near East, Arabia and North Africa. Mainly

Below: The leopard's dappled coat blends perfectly with the surrounding vegetation.

Opposite: Cheetah mother and young.

Opposite: Cheetah cubs ready to start their own life.

solitary, it moves at night and is equally at home on the ground or in trees. So slender and flexible is the body of the genet it can follow its head through any opening.

The **Large Spotted (or Bush) Genet**, longer than the more common small-spotted genet, lacks a dorsal crest, has shorter fur and larger body spots. Widespread throughout Kenya, it favours woodland and forest habitats.

Genet spend their day in rock crevices, hollow trees or drowsing on a large branch. They return to the same place day after day, hunting mostly on the ground, only climbing trees to raid nests. Young are born two or three to a litter. Genet spit and growl like cats when angry or threatened. Their normal call is a clear, metallic note.

Kenya's six or seven varieties of mongoose are pert, attractive little creatures of the underbrush, tremendously brave and ferocious. Together with an innate swiftness, this makes them a match for even the swiftest of striking snakes, the cobra and the mamba.

The **Dwarf Mongoose**, smallest of Kenya's species, is active during the day. This friendly diminutive moves about in packs of up to fifteen kinfolk, looking for grubs, insects, larvae, spiders, small rodents, reptiles, eggs, and young birds as food. They attack live prey *en masse*, swooping down on the victims with a savage growl.

Stockily-built, with a short snout and speckled brown or reddish-brown coat, they live in dry savannah woodlands – taking refuge in old termite hills, rock crevices, or hollow trees. Nomadic, with little concern for their own safety; they are

frequently seen. They communicate with a wide vocabulary of bird-like chirrups and whistles.

Perhaps the best known of Kenya's mongoose family, and the largest, is the **Large Grey Mongoose**. Greyish-brown with a long and relatively slender tail ending in a black tuft, it was revered by the ancient Egyptians as a God-like creature. Seen from a distance, when walking single file in a group, this train often looks like a giant, undulating snake.

They are found everywhere in Kenya, particularly along the edges of lakes and swamplands, woodlands, and thick bush. Widespread throughout Africa, mongoose are also found in southern Spain and Israel. They live in old aardvark burrows, crevices, or hollow trees.

Another species common throughout Kenya, from the most remote woodlands to the fallow farmland of densely-settled areas, the **Slender (Black Tipped) Mongoose** is often mistaken for a ground squirrel when running. It holds its tail up straight just like that creature.

Probably the most frequently seen of all mongooses, their coats are a deep reddish-brown with long black-tipped tails. Active both day and night, though basically ground animals, they climb trees – feeding on rodents, reptiles, snakes, birds, eggs, insects, larvae, and fruit. Born two to four to a litter in hollow trees or holes in the ground, these delightful animals are easily tamed and make wonderful pets.

Large, thickset, with a grey coat of shaggy hair and the white tail from which it derives its name, the **White Tailed Mongoose** varies its behaviour according to its habitat. Basically a night

29

Below: Serval, a nocturnal cat that is seldom seen.

Opposite: Genet, frequent raiders of poultry houses.

Opposite: Mongooses.

animal of the ground, in some areas it moves into the trees during the day.

They are the heaviest of the mongoose, favouring almost any kind of environment from wooded areas, bush and even open plains, to locations close to water where they add molluscs and crabs to their universal diet of small animals, frogs, rodents, reptiles, and insects. When angry they communicate with a loud and threatening bark.

Of medium size, with transverse dark-coloured bands along its greyish-brown body, the **Banded Mongoose** moves around in packs of up to a dozen. Never far from water, it is found in many kinds of habitat except dense forest. Highly social, the groups often grow in size until they number between thirty and fifty gregarious and loveable creatures.

They spend much of their six-year life span in noisy packs. The strident, twittering cries of this cheerful rabble are the only clues to the origins of what, from a distance, appears to be some never-ending serpent weaving through the bush.

When threatened these delightful animals growl and spit like cats. They make wonderful pets and frequently put down snakes and other unwanted pests; detecting them with their sharp eyes, keen hearing and excellent sense of smell.

2. Wild Dogs and Others

Few animals are blessed with as much social spirit as that of the **Wild Dog**. These 'Wolves of Africa' display a wonderful sense of community. They live and hunt in packs – from as few as ten to as many as 100 – with remarkable success. Wild dogs can sustain a pace of forty-eight kilometres an hour for almost two kilometres. When one is exhausted another takes its place in the chase. The pack eats on the run, tearing the flesh off the luckless prey while it is in flight, often ripping out its entrails until it drops exhausted. A pack of twelve can consume a full-grown impala within ten minutes.

There is some reprieve for the antelope and gazelle which make up most of their diet. The pack hunts only at sunup and sundown, between 6.30 and 7.00 in the morning and from 6.00 to 7.30 in the evening. A pack's kill averages just under two kilos of flesh a day for each animal.

These social and affectionate animals take great care of their young, feeding them with semi-digested meat which the adults regurgitate. The lame and sick which trail after the hunt are cared for, too. When they come upon the kill they are made welcome to the feast. Colleagues will regurgitate for them also.

The young treat their seniors with deference. Those that do not are chastised with a snapping bite on the flank. This makes the youngster freeze, raise its head and whimper obedience. Among each other, wild dogs are gentle and persuasive, licking faces and muzzles, and crouching in deference whenever they want something from another member of the pack, usually meat or company.

Opposite: Silver-backed jackal.

Below: Wild dog, perhaps the most sociable of
Africa's wild animals.

Wild dogs, which range far and wide throughout Kenya, have little fear of man to whom they are indifferent. One pack was seen by a climbing party at the very summit – 5,895 metres – of Africa's highest mountain, Kilimanjaro.

Kenya's jackals, with their slender long legs, look more like domestic dogs and, in fact, are fairly closely related to them.

The **Black-backed (or silver-backed) Jackal** is the most common of the Kenyan jackals distinguished by the broad black band, similar to that of a German Shepherd (Alsatian) dog, which runs along its back, and white underbelly. Resourceful animals, they hunt and scavenge, in packs of as many as thirty, on small antelope up to the size of a Thomson's gazelle, hares, rodents, guinea fowl and other ground birds, reptiles, eggs, and insects. They swoop down on a kill with an unmistakable siren-like howl – darting in and out among the feasting lion or cheetah, snatching titbits from under their noses. They are also prey themselves for lion, leopard, and python. Cubs are often taken by eagles.

The most elusive of the three species is the **Side-Striped Jackal**, moving stealthily through the undergrowth at night. Essentially a scavenger, it gets its name from the indistinct light stripe along its flank.

The **Golden Jackal**, adaptable to changing circumstances and environment, has been found living close to villages, large towns and even in the suburbs of Nairobi, where it scavenges on garbage dumps at night.

With its appealing face and gigantic ears, the **Bat-eared Fox** is one of Kenya's most endearing creatures. In shape and appearance it could have been crafted by a Walt Disney artist.

Its enormous ears provide acutely-tuned antennae for picking up the location of the insects on which it feeds. This sensitive listening system also acts as defence. The bat-eared fox, which is active at night spends the day drowsing outside its burrow, yet ever alert, its ears twitching left or right. When danger threatens it flattens them close against the side of its face.

The Bat-eared Fox which mates for life is the only one of the seven African foxes found in Kenya. As with most of these small creatures, zoologists have not paid much attention to the bat-eared fox. But its plaintive cry is perhaps a poignant expression of its fate, like that of the rest of its kin, as one of nature's constant and furtive fugitives.

While some animals have suffered seriously from poaching and hunting, hyaena have prospered, as they have never been a target of the hunter or poacher. Indeed, though for many years considered only as scavengers, they are themselves ruthless and successful hunters. Dog-like in appearance and behaviour – male hyaena cock their leg to urinate – hyaena are probably more closely related to the mongoose.

Spotted Hyaena hunt in packs of up to thirty. Their range of prey is varied and their appetite indiscriminate. They cut down wildebeest, zebra and gazelle at speeds of up to sixty-four kilometres an hour. These voracious killers follow pregnant

Below: The bat-eared fox's large ears enable it to detect possible danger – and small prey.

Opposite: Hyaena on a wildebeest kill.

Opposite: Hyaena chases vultures off carrion.

females, snatching their new-born as they are delivered. Their strong teeth and powerful jaws allow hyaena to crack bones easily, sucking out what is to them the delectable marrow. Given the opportunity, spotted hyaena attack humans and, not infrequently, their own kind.

Almost any form of food – from rubbish tip scavengings to fleet-footed Thomson's gazelle – is grist to the hyaena's all-consuming mill. They have been seen eating brooms, old shoes, and bicycle saddles. But live prey forms about eighty per cent of their diet – making them more efficient hunters than the lion which will often eat the hyaena's leftovers.

Coal-black, the cubs are born with eyes wide open, teeth cut, and can walk at once. Their life expectancy is up to forty years. Like dogs and wolves, hyaena bay at the moon. But instead of throwing their heads back, they point their muzzles down. The spotted hyaena, which prefers bush and wooded country, lush rolling grasslands, forest and mountain slope, is seen almost everywhere. The **Striped Hyaena**, a smaller animal, is found in dry, stunted plains.

Nature has been unkind to the **Aardwolf**. Its behaviour is far from wolfish. Though it may occasionally pounce on a passing rodent, it is an ill-equipped killer and has few defences against attack. When frightened, it raises its distinctive back mane to make itself look much bigger. If it is actually attacked, it gives off a strong and repugnant smell like a skunk.

Its sandy brown coat, marked by dark vertical stripes, makes it

look like a more elegant miniature of the striped hyaena, to which it may be distantly related. Although some experts think the aardwolf is unique, many suggest it is a form of hyaena which, through a changing diet over the centuries, has degenerated into a family by itself.

The chances of seeing one are rare, anyway. They move about by night, hiding during the daytime in old aardvark burrows in which they raise their young, usually three to a litter, often in small communities of nursing females.

Below: Baboons also display a strong sense of community.

Opposite: Black and white colobus monkey, perhaps the loveliest of all Africa's primates.

3. Monkeys

Kenya's two species of baboon, with their distinctive, long, dog-like faces, also uncannily 'ape' many of the characteristics of the canine species, including their bark, their preference for walking on all four limbs, unlike most other primates, and their carnivorous habits. For although basically vegetarian, meat forms a consistent, if limited, part of their food.

The larger of the two, the **Olive Baboon**, is also the more common, found everywhere in Kenya but the east, where the **Yellow Baboon**, smaller in height, is dominant. They cover up to eighteen kilometres a day in a constant search for food – shoots, roots, seeds, bushes, flowers, insects – and an occasional kill. They prey on timid mammals – hares and young gazelle – whose defence is to 'freeze' to the ground. They also snatch up fledgling birds.

Baboon normally use trees only to escape danger and to sleep. They never walk upright, but move forward on all fours. Extremely social, their well-organized groups are known as troops and average between forty and eighty animals. Each troop is permanent, ruled by a dominant male which assumed authority by force. When it becomes senile, a younger leader usurps its place in a vicious battle for power.

Baboon are fierce fighters, and predators regard them with respect. When an enemy is sighted the troop leaders give the alarm, barking until the females and the young are surrounded by mature escorts – a primitive praetorian guard of snarling, snapping hostility. They are well-equipped for defence, with acute hearing and eyesight allied to extremely effective teeth. They often inflict severe, sometimes fatal, wounds on their enemy.

Females become sexually receptive about one week in every

four. They mate indiscriminately and frequently, first with the meeker males and then the more dominant ones. Youngsters, born black with red faces, are carried under the belly. Later, like young jockeys, they move to a 'horse-riding' position on the back. These early months are an important introduction to the intricate rituals and behaviour of the troop's social structures.

Few sights in the wild are more graceful than a **Black and White Colobus** monkey on the move. As it leaps through the topmost levels of the forest with its fur and tail spread out like a vibrant cape it appears to glide. But, seen in silhouette, it is distinctly pot-bellied.

Colobus differ from most other monkeys in two respects. They have only four digits on either hand – there is no thumb – and they spend virtually their entire lives above ground, in the highest levels of the forest. Rarely, if ever, do colobus monkeys come down to earth. Few creatures can equal their climbing ability or their leap – as much as thirty metres. They differ, too, from most other monkeys in their capacity to remain silent, often for hours on end.

These animals have been ruthlessly hunted for their fabulous coats. It is the badge of office of senior elders of the Kikuyu. Colobus, which live in troops of up to twenty-five animals made up of several family groups, are the most specialized feeders of all monkeys – living on a selective diet of forest leaves. Occasionally, when desperate, they eat insects. Much has yet to be discovered about this fascinating and lovely-to-look-at primate.

Another family of high-living monkeys belongs to the *Guenon* group of tree-dwelling, daytime creatures confined to the tropical forest – with one exception. The **Black-faced Vervet (or**

Below and opposite: Colourful but rare de Brazza monkeys.

Green) monkey has developed in the opposite direction and has branched out to live down on the savannah. The only monkey of its kind with a black face, there are many variations throughout Kenya of this versatile and highly adaptable animal.

They use the gallery forests and thick bush for refuge and sleep, but forage widely on the open ground, often over long distances – up to 400 to 500 metres – in troops of between six to twenty, although groups of up to 100 have been observed. Mainly vegetarian, they feed on a diet of leaves, young shoots, bark, flowers, fruits, bulbs, roots and grass seeds for most of their twenty- to twenty-four-year life spans. The also augment this with insects, grubs, caterpillars, spiders, eggs, young ground birds like guinea fowl and francolin and, in rare instances, rodents or hares.

Vervets have acute vision and excellent hearing but a poor sense of smell. They communicate with a wide range of facial expressions, lowering eyebrows, raising and jerking heads, and threaten with bared teeth and wide open mouth. If a newly born infant is held by an alien it provokes a violent reaction from any adult vervet, stimulating rescue initiatives which include threat displays.

The genitalia of both the vervet and the **Patas** monkey are an incredible, iridescent sky-blue that signals sexual identity and interest. But the Patas is the only primate which never mixes with other monkeys. Because of its colouring and shape it is also known as the **Red Hussar**.

This large, tall and long-legged monkey lives almost exclusively on the ground and can stand and walk, fully erect, on its hind legs. It uses trees – and termite hills – as vantage points. The Patas weighs up to ten kilos. Known as the 'greyhound of the apes', it has been clocked at fifty-six kilometres an hour. Patas, which avoid dense cover and favour very dry savannah, are found around Nanyuki, Rumuruti, Eldoret, Kitale, and the Kongelai Escarpment and West Pokot.

The **Sykes** monkey, with its distinct white throat and chest patch, is a member of the **Blue** monkey races which are larger and rather stout. They hold their thick long tails, with a slightly curved tip, higher than the body when walking.

Sykes have narrow, elongated faces with a purplish-black tone, no beards, but dense, bristly tufts of hair on their foreheads, earning them also the name of **Diadem**. Moving their black legs in a distinctive, gentle, trotting gait, Sykes' monkeys are found wherever there are forests.

Sykes are related to the extremely rare and beautiful **Golden** monkey, distinguished by their greenish-gold backs merging to orange on their flanks, which live in limited numbers in isolated pockets in western Kenya.

Resident in the Cherangani Hills, the **de Brazza** monkey, pale blue-grey with black limbs, an orange forehead, and white breast, is another of Kenya's colourful but rare primates, as is the **Grey (or Mangabey)**, found only in the Lower Tana Primate Reserve.

With its big, bright, wide-open, childlike eyes and the call of a baby's cry, it's no surprise that the **Lesser Galago**, a nocturnal primate, is better known as the **Bushbaby**. This delightful, endearing creature, small, slim-built with thick and woolly fur, has a conspicuous white stripe down its nose. It is widespread and common throughout Kenya. Bushbabies, which hide elusively in coastal bush and acacia woodlands and forests, make delightful pets.

Below: The delightful bushbaby spends much of
its time in trees.

Right: Vervet monkey, one of the primates that forage on open ground.

Right: Syke's monkey, commonly found in Kenya's forests.

Bushbabies are well-adapted to life in the trees. Their tail acting as a weight, they use their hind legs to grasp the branches before leap-frogging from one branch to another. They sometimes come to the ground where they walk upright, or in a crouch, leaping occasionally on their extremely powerful hind legs like a tiny kangaroo. Bushbabies can jump an incredible three metres. They have a large vocabulary – at least eight different calls, including a high-pitched alarm call which they can keep up for an hour or more. Litters usually number two, born in a nest prepared by the mother, which leaves the young behind during her nightly search for food.

Although they are related, there could be no greater contrast to the impish liveliness of the bushbaby than the **Pottos**. These little, bear-like animals have no tail – or, at least, only a rudimentary stump, rounded head, small ears and unequal limbs.

The Pottos, known in many an African vernacular as 'half-a-tail', live exclusively in the top storeys of their forest home – rarely, if ever, coming down to earth. It would, indeed, be difficult for them to do so. The movements of these cuddly-looking, slow motion 'teddy bear'-like creatures are as close to active inertia as the law of physics and description allow.

Found in Kenya only in the Kakamega Forest, they are easily located at night by shining a powerful torch into their reflective, always astonished eyes.

4. The Antelopes – Large

Among those cast in the role of prey in nature are the ox-like wild ruminants which browse or graze in a wide range of habitats. Better known as antelope or gazelle, they are normally shy, easily startled and, not surprisingly, always alert. Fully mature, the **Eland**, the heavyweight of Kenya's fragile pastures, weighs close to a tonne. Few could imagine such a massive animal has anything to fear from predators. Yet lion frequently slay this placid bovid.

So perhaps more astonishing then, is not its part as a link in the predatory food chain, but its ability, virtually from a standing position, to leap a height of more than two metres.

Between 1.7 to 1.8 metres at the shoulder, they are the largest of Kenya's antelope. Their large twisted horns average around seventy-six centimetres long – the record length being more than one metre. These horns are important for feeding. To collect twigs, they grasp them between the two pedicles (or stalks), breaking them loose with a shake of their head and powerful neck.

For all their size and weight, their powerful chest hidden behind the large and pendulous dewlap, eland are graceful creatures, well-proportioned and elegantly symmetrical.

Common in Kenya in most areas south of the Tana River, eland gather in herds ranging from a few animals up to 200; occasionally much larger. They often mix with zebra. Old bulls live away from the herds on their own. Their life span is from fifteen to twenty years.

Despite their size, they are easily tamed. With less fat than beef cattle, they have been domesticated for meat and milk. This process began as early as the 19th century when one founding herd was transported to Russia where eland, herded by Ukranian cowboys, still graze the steppes.

Above: Rare greater kudu, distinguished by its magnificent lyrate antlers.

Opposite: Eland, the largest of Africa's antelope.

Right: Female kudu.

Weighing between 272 to 317 kilos, **Greater Kudu** can also easily clear two metres at a jump despite their impressive weight. Distinguished by what are among the most magnificent horns in the antelope kingdom, their spiral antlers average around 1.3 metres long, with the record length a fraction under 1.8 metres. Their acute hearing is accentuated by their ability to turn their large rounded ears in almost any direction. These large, slender, and elegant antelopes, grey in colour with six to eight prominent vertical white stripes on either flank, raise their tail when alarmed – the white underside serving as a warning.

Kudu live out their twelve to fifteen years in small herds or families of four to five, although herds of thirty have been seen. In Kenya they are found on many of the rocky, arid hill slopes in the north, along the precipitous sides of the Rift Valley, between Lakes Bogoria and Turkana, and in the area between Mount Suswa and Lake Magadi and the Nkuruman Escarpment. These antelopes, once rare in Kenya, have made something of a comeback from the rinderpest epidemic which almost wiped them out at the turn of the century.

The **Lesser Kudu**, a smaller, more graceful version of the Greater, displays more stripes – between eleven and fifteen – down the flank. They prefer much drier country and can go without water for a long time. They are widespread in eastern and northern Kenya.

Nothing in the antelope world emulates the run of the **Bongo**, a shy night-time antelope of the mountain forests. It goes into a crouching position and throws up its head, the horns lying flat along its back. In the thick tangle of thicket, trees, and bamboo groves in which it lives, this allows it to move swiftly through the undergrowth. An elusive creature, it is the largest of Kenya's forest antelopes.

Its bright chestnut coat has twelve to fourteen vertical white stripes – fewer than its western African counterpart – down the flanks. With age, the coat darkens.

Unwilling jumpers, they are shy and easily disturbed. Bongo are browsers, feeding on leaves, shoots of shrubs, and creepers. Rotten wood and bark is a favoured delicacy. They live in pairs and groups of up to thirty to thirty-five, but old bulls quit the herd to live out the end of their twelve- to fourteen-year life span on their own. They are found in the Aberdare, Mount Kenya, and Mau forests, but are rarely seen. They may recently have become extinct in the Cherangani Hills.

The **Sitatunga**, though similar to the bongo, is unique among antelopes and easily distinguished. For it is a remarkable example of nature's virtuosity. The sitatunga has evolved so that its two-toed, elongated hooves on either foot spread widely to dissipate its weight, which enables it to move about on mats of floating weeds, and appear to walk on water.

Sitatungas have truly amphibious habits. Alarmed, they sink into the water, only the tip of their nostrils showing. Known, too, as marshbuck, sitatungas also swim adeptly. Mainly a night antelope, browsing on leaves, twigs, fruits, and tender grass, they live alone or in pairs, sometimes in occasional herds of up to fifteen, for about twelve years. They bark when alarmed and communicate by bleating. The only place they can be seen in Kenya is in the tiny Saiwa National Park, not far from Kitale, near the Cherangani Hills, where the wildlife authorities have thoughtfully provided tree-top platforms from which visitors can watch them.

Though *aficionados* of the bush have long relished venison – chops of Thomson's Gazelle, marinated, are a speciality of the house in one of Nairobi's international hotels – few would

Opposite: Bongo, a rare nocturnal antelope, distinguished by its striped flanks.

Above: Defassa waterbuck are distinguished from the common waterbuck by their pure white rump.

bother with **Waterbuck**. To skin these creatures requires a skill denied most butchers or hunters. The skins have scent glands which give off an unpleasant musky smell so powerful that, long after they have left, it serves as a tell-tale indication of their previous presence. And unless exceptional care is taken in dressing, this musk taints the waterbuck meat making it unpalatable.

But waterbuck are elegant antelope. Their majestic horns are unmistakable. Around an average of seventy centimetres long, the record length is a fraction over one metre. With a short, glossy coat, brown to greyish-brown, the **Common Waterbuck** is distinct from its kindred race, the **Defassa Waterbuck**, because of the white crescent across the rump. The Defassa has pure white buttocks. Waterbuck, which are grazers, are found in woodlands, flood plains, and clearings, usually close to water. But although they frequently hide in it, they are truly land animals.

Seen from the side, poised and alert before bounding away, it is easy to imagine the **Oryx** as the mythical unicorn. In profile the splendid horns merge as one to match exactly the images drawn so long ago in the Middle Ages. Long and slender-looking, these are powerful weapons of both defence and attack, a bit like the duellist's épée, well-suited to a challenge to the death in the dusty drylands, as many a lion has found to its cost.

Heads down between their forelegs, oryx wield their very long horns with dexterity in the savage cut and thrust of the wild, often impaling their victims with such force the horns pass clean through the body. The horns average about seventy centimetres, with a record length of more than a metre.

Some experts suggest that the distinctive black and white

facial markings of the oryx actually serve as a warning to predators to steer clear. Usually seen in groups of between ten and twelve, oryx live out their twelve to fifteen years on a varied diet of grass, plants, leaves, shoots, wild melons, succulent roots, tubers, and bulbs. These grazers can go long periods without water. Unlike most other antelopes they do not jump often – though they can do so with prodigious power when needed – preferring to creep under obstacles rather than leap over them.

The **Beisa Oryx** are found in Kenya north of the Tana. The **Fringe-eared Oryx**, marked by the distinctive tassel on the end of their ears, and heavier and rather brown coats, are found south of the Tana.

Red-brown skin glowing with iridescent sheen, that lumpy-looking creature standing solitary guard on a mound is the **Topi**, familiar sentinel in Kenya's Maasai Mara. The burnished skin seems almost the result of too liberal an application of polish. For a creature killed as often as the topi, the sentinel is a necessity. This prolific species, to a lesser degree than the wildebeest, forms part of nature's greatest spectacle, the annual migration from Serengeti into the Mara, and is prime flesh for all the predators which follow the migration, particularly savoured by the lion.

Large and robust, the shoulders of the topi are noticeably higher than their rump, giving them the familiar hartebeest look. An overall reddish-brown to purplish-red, they have distinct dark patches on their face, upper forehead, legs, hips, and thighs.

Jousting males, each of which has its own territory, drop to their knees and clash horns. Rutting males mark out their territory with dung heaps and by rubbing facial and foot glands

Below: Rapier-like horns of the oryx often inflict fatal wounds on predators.

Opposite: Topi, one of the hartebeest family, with coat of burnished copper.

Opposite: Hartebeest, also known as kongoni, distinguished by its massive shoulders and sloping back.

on the ground. They then take guard on the nearest high ground, usually an old termite mound.

Pure grazers, they can go without water for a long time if grass is green. They also eat grasses disdained by other antelope. They are swift runners, making off with a bounding gait. Topi are found in the Mara, and north of the Tana River and east of Lake Turkana. The related species, **Tiang**, occur on Lake Turkana's north-westernmost shores.

Much topi behaviour also characterizes the **Hartebeest**. Males keep watch from knolls or high ground after defining their territory and winning the courtship battle for a harem. But for a good part of their twelve to fifteen years, hartebeest bulls are celibate. The losers form bachelor herds and old bulls are cast out to live a solitary existence until they die.

The most common, **Coke's Hartebeest**, is around 1.2 metres high at the shoulder, and weighs around sixty-two to ninety kilos. Two other species are **Jackson's** and **Hunter's**; the former being larger, the latter smaller.

The long head, with the massive brow which looks like a wall plaque, forms an ideal setting for the dramatic horns – the Coke's averaging just over thirty-five centimetres. The record length for this species is just under sixty centimetres. Sandy fawn in colour, the hump-shouldered hartebeests wander around looking completely out of proportion. Their long heads and massive brows give them a doltish look. Placid, except when rutting, hartebeest bulls snort when alarmed.

Coke's are widespread in southern Kenya. Jackson's are found only in the extreme north-west and Hunter's, unmistakable because of the shape of their horns and the white chevron between the eyes, occur between the Tana River and Somalia. One small group has been translocated to Tsavo National Park.

Nature's design department appears to have suffered an overload when the planning schedule came to the **Wildebeest**. Nothing in Kenya's animal kingdom comes remotely close to emulating this patchwork-quilt of a creature.

Given the front of an ox, the face of a jester, the beard of a mandarin, the rear of an antelope, and the tail of a horse, not for nothing is it called the 'clown of the plains'. Its character is as woolly and insane as its design. Yet, without a doubt, it is the star of the world's greatest animal spectacular – the annual migration from Serengeti to the Maasai Mara.

More than a million of these strange looking creatures, joined by zebra and topi, march from the lush grasslands of southern Serengeti in Tanzania to the northernmost corner of the Mara's rolling grasslands. They follow the rains and the pasture in a display as instinctive, and often as suicidal, as that of the lemming of Norway.

Thousands of wildebeest swarm behind their leaders into the swollen rivers in such numbers that many hundreds die. Their bloated carcasses sustain abundant numbers of crocodile. On the hoof, they provide a veritable banquet for the predators which wax abundant on the fat pickings of the migration. Not surprisingly. With a weight between 159 and 220 kilos, the wildebeest is a meal on its own.

The young, born a reddish-brown fawn, can stand within five minutes of birth and take on their mature colour after two months. The wildebeest habit of moving in single-file formation make them unique among plains game. Extremely gregarious, non-migrational herds number up to 150 females and young, herded by one to three bulls which trot around the herd in their peculiar, head-high, rocking gait, forcing the herd into a tight mass. Wildebeest bulls defend their territory even on the move,

making a continuous cacaphony of low, moaning grunts and explosive snorts.

They scatter during the rains and in the dry season cover up to fifty kilometres a day to find water. Their diet is almost entirely grass. Inhabiting open grassy plains and thorn bush, typical of the Mara, they are abundant throughout southern Kenya and can usually be seen in Nairobi National Park.

There's a touch of unmistakable aristocracy about the **Roan Antelope** male, third largest of Kenya's antelopes. From an early age, the rare roan is an aggressive animal, with weapons to match their temper. The horns of the male on average are seventy centimetres long. The roan depends almost entirely on grass throughout its fifteen-year life span, living in herds of up to twenty. Rutting males joust with rivals by going down on their knees and making sweeping movements of the horns. In Kenya they are found only on the shores of Lake Victoria at Lambwe Valley, and in the trans-Mara region. Some were translocated from the Ithanga hills, far inland in the Ukambani, to the Shimba Hills at the Coast. But they did not thrive.

It is in the Shimba Hills, however, that Kenya's only remaining **Sable** antelope, similar to the roan but slightly smaller, can be found. The sable is one of the most beautiful of the larger antelopes, the male's satin-like coat appearing almost pure black, the female's a dark reddish-brown.

Sable prefer woodlands to open plains, but the open grasslands and ancient forests of the Shimba Hills provide a perfect environment.

5. The Antelopes – Small

If for nothing else, **Grant's Gazelle** is distinguished in that it immortalizes a little-known Scotsman. James Augustus Grant was thirty-three when he joined Speke's expedition in search of the Nile 1860 and, though he was the first to record the gazelle which bears his name, curiously he never saw the source of the Nile. When Speke came upon it, Grant remained behind in the permanent camp. He died in 1892 and is recalled for little else other than the gazelle which carries his name.

More curious is the fact that Grant's gazelle is a positive lexicon of early European exploration in Africa. A subspecies is **Roberts's Gazelle**, named after Frederick Sleigh Roberts, who won the Victoria Cross in India in 1858, later led the relief of Mafeking and became the first Earl Roberts of Kandaha, Pretoria and Waterford.

Other subspecies are **Bright's Gazelle** and **Peters' Gazelle**. Although little concerning Bright but his name is left to posterity, Peters has a large place in the colonial history of East Africa. A German mercenary, Karl Peters led the race to annex that area of the region which is now Uganda and Tanzania.

Both grazers and browsers, Grant's gazelles can endure extreme heat and go without water for long periods during their ten to twelve years of life. Moving about throughout most of an active day, rarely seeking shade, they form herds varying in size from six to thirty, usually with a male in charge of a harem of about a dozen does. Their call is an alarmed grunt or bleat. Thomson's gazelles are their smaller look-alikes and they are often found together on the Maasai plains. The only certain way of telling them apart is that in Grant's the white on the buttocks reaches above the tail and in Thomson's it ends below the root of the tail.

It should come as no surprise to know that **Thomson's**

Below: Powerful sable antelope.

Opposite: Grant's gazelle, which takes its name from a little-known Scottish companion of Speke.

Gazelle is also named after an explorer – the man, perhaps, who is the best known of all Kenya's white visitors of the last century. Joseph Thomson's name is particularly associated with the country after his epic march in 1883-84 through Maasailand which resulted in a best-selling adventure yarn of the Victorian era.

Their short stumpy tails rotating in perpetual motion, Thomson's gazelles are flesh for almost every predator – and, where their ranges coincide, the cheetah's basic diet. Grass forms about ninety per cent of their diet, and herbs make up the other ten per cent.

Thomson's gazelle like to drink daily, but when the grass is lush can go without water. They have no alarm call. Instead, they signal danger by rippling or flexing the muscles in their flanks. They can leap incredibly high in a stiff-legged, standing-still jump known as 'stotting' or 'pronking'.

Females, which have smaller horns, breed all the year so that sometimes they may give birth to two fawns in twelve months. Both young and adult have the ability to 'freeze' in an absolutely prone position – even the chin extending horizontally along the ground – when threatened.

There is little in nature to equal the flawless economy of movement, symmetry, proportion, and blend of colour which the **Impala** embodies. The emblematic species of the East African Wildlife Society is also food for almost every large predator, yet continues to maintain itself in large populations.

One reason is their habit of breaking into prodigious leaps when threatened. Taking off in a series of soaring bounds, spectacularly beautiful to watch, they jump obstacles towering three metres above the ground or leap ditches up to ten metres wide. Changing direction upon each landing, their zig-zag course disconcerts any predator.

Set above a profile of deceptively simple beauty, their distinctive lyrate-shaped horns average just over thirty centimetres, with a record length of around a metre. Their crowning glories, however, are their eyes and rumps. No beautician could have conceived anything more seductive than the delicate streak of white above each eye, and the gentle brushwork of lighter shading just below. Two white patches, beneath the nostrils and above the mouth, with a shading of white beneath, complete the picture.

White buttocks are framed on either side with vertical black lines down each thigh. A prominent black stripe down the white tail, ending in a white tuft, provides a finishing touch of symmetrical contrast almost without equal in nature's colouring book. They do not carry black stripes along the flank. Unique among antelope, with little 'socks' of black hair on the ankles just above the heels of the hind legs, impalas are all grace, power, and vulnerability.

Active both day and night, they browse throughout their twelve years on leaves, bushes, short grass, and fruits. They drink dew and in some, but not all, areas can survive without visible sources of water. Impala range over acacia savannah and light woodlands in south-western and central Kenya.

Were it not for nature's artistic eye, the **Bushbuck**, though small and appealing, would arouse little interest. But its dappled white markings are a perfect example of natural camouflage. Blending into rock and bush, this shy, mainly nocturnal creature of forest and thicket flits elusively in and out of cover. Bushbuck need their camouflage to avoid their principal enemy, the leopard.

When cornered or wounded they defend themselves and

Below: Thomson's gazelle.

Opposite: The unique klipspringer negotiates its
rocky homeland with ease.

their young with considerable courage. Their short bushy tails are white underneath. Raised on the run, they serve as a warning beacon for others.

Mainly nocturnal, they spend most of their twelve to fifteen years alone or in small groups, browsing on leaves, shoots, acacia pods, tubers and roots, only eating the first flush of young grass. They communicate with a loud bark, a bit like that of the baboon, and also in a range of grunts.

Always close to thick cover, bushbuck are widespread in southern Kenya, the Aberdares, Mount Kenya, Marsabit, Mount Kulal and other isolated mountain forests.

Though a day creature, the **Bohor Reedbuck** is an elusive antelope, shy and easily startled, normally seen at sunup and sundown. These small, graceful antelope lie up during the day in reed beds or tall grasses, shaping the stems around them into a shelter. Alarmed, they go down onto the ground in a squatting position – only bolting at the last moment. They run with a peculiar gait – like animated rocking horses suddenly brought to life.

The short horns of the reedbuck – hunted by all the large predators – provide little defence. An average of less than thirty centimetres, the record length is under forty-five centimetres. Sometimes solitary, they normally move around in pairs or small family groups, with young males forming bachelor herds of no more than three to four. The Bohor reedbuck is widespread in southern Kenya west of the Tana River.

The other, **Chanler's Mountain Reedbuck**, very similar but slightly larger, is found in central and western Kenya on open grassed hill slopes up to 4,000 metres.

Not much bigger than a rabbit, the delicate and fragile **Dik-dik** is the 'Tom Thumb' of all Kenya's *Beautiful Animals* – a gentle, greyish fawn darting through the thickets in shy and elusive flight around twilight. Their locations are easily identified by the middens which they establish – up to a metre in diameter – in pairs to mark the boundaries of their territory.

Two species live in Kenya but are seen only briefly. Stalked and harried by almost every predator including baboon, these tiny, shin-high antelopes have an elfin charm which only serves to emphasize their vulnerability.

Kirk's Dik-diks, their hindquarters taller than their front shoulders and with long, thin legs and sloping back, look permanently startled. They are the most common and roam dry and arid lands even where the trees are very scattered – as long as there is enough ground undergrowth for refuge. Extremely territorial, they rarely wander far, remaining in one small district and always moving about on the same pathways. Normally they live in pairs and occasionally form small family groups. Dik-diks feed throughout their five to ten years of life on leaves, shoots, fruits, roots, and tubers. They can go without water indefinitely.

In flight, they run in a series of zig-zag bounds. Their alarm call is a shrill whistle, a bit like a bird call – or a *zik-zik* cry – hence their name. The **Guenther's Long-snouted Dik-dik** is found in northern Kenya.

Unique among antelope, the **Klipspringer** is the 'chamois' of Kenya. It almost seems able to walk up the precipitous rock faces in the craggy regions in which it lives.

Measuring around fifty-one to fifty-six centimetres high from hoof to shoulder, and weighing between eleven and eighteen kilos, the klipspringer is a phenomenal jumper as well. It bounces on the tips of its rubbery hooves as it walks, making its exceptionally strong legs look even longer – the tip-toe effect accentuating the impression.

Below: Impala, perhaps the loveliest of Africa's antelope.

Opposite: Bushbuck live in a wide range of habitats.

Opposite: Bohor reedbuck, never found far from water.

Unlike the coat of any other African antelope, the olive yellow coat, speckled with grey, is stiff and brittle, serving as a cushion to ward off the shocks of hitting rock walls when they jump.

Living only in rocky hills, klipspringers, like most other antelope, mark their territories with a secretion from their scent glands. They graze on herbs and shrubs and drink water when it is available, but can draw enough of their liquid needs from their food.

Bounding along at speed, occasionally leaping high into the air, the **Oribi** is sometimes mistaken for a duiker or reedbuck. It is another of Kenya's beautiful small antelopes, with a long slender neck and silky coat.

With a colour that varies from pale fawn grey to bright reddish-brown, oribi are distinguished by the bare, black glandular patches below their large, oval-shaped ears. Their short tails, which have a black tip, are raised when running.

Almost totally grazers, spending the day in long grass or light bush, oribi live in pairs or small parties and when alarmed give shrill loud whistles or sneezes. They leap straight up in the air in a stiff-legged, standing-still jump before bounding off. Some experts suggest that this way they can scan a larger area of bush for signs of predators.

Head held high, running swiftly, the elegant little **Steinbok** (or Steenbok) often eludes its predators by suddenly darting down into an old aardvark burrow which, in more placid times, the females may also use to raise their young. Slim and slender – found from sea level up to the 4,500-metre contour of Kenya's mountain regions – these delicate red-brown to fawn creatures are all poetry in motion.

Steinboks have a black crescent patch between their horns and a smaller one on the nose. Their belly and buttocks are pure white and the coat sometimes greyish with a light, silvery sheen.

Living alone, pairing only during the mating season, steinbok are both browsers and grazers with a wide range of food and the ability to survive without water. They avoid hilly country but are often found in sand dunes, particularly at the Kenya Coast.

The **Gerenuk** spends a great deal of its life on its hind legs, searching for the lusher leaves found high up on the acacia thorns and other desert shrubs on which it survives. These unique antelope were only discovered to zoology as recently as 1878.

Their name derives from the Somali language meaning 'giraffe-necked'. As it has learned to use its rear legs to stand in a vertical posture while feeding, so its neck has evolved through the milleniums to become longer and longer. Antelope of the desert, gerenuk survive without water, drawing all the liquid they need from their diet. During extreme drought, however, one animal has been observed to drink the urine of another.

Browsing on tender leaves, shoots, prickly bushes and trees, seldom grazing, except after exceptional rains, gerenuk roam the badlands north of Tanzania's Pare Mountains all through eastern Kenya but are frequently seen at their best in the Samburu reserve.

These elegant creatures are also fascinating when they run. Extremely swift, they bring their long necks down in line with their slender backs, and suddenly – because of the extreme length of their stride – appear to have shrunk to about half their height.

The **Suni**, no taller than thirty-one centimetres and only eight kilos in weight, is rarely seen. It moves mostly at sunup and sundown. But it leaves one tell-tale clue to its presence – a strong, musky scent which lingers, like that of the waterbuck, long after it has left a location.

Mainly browsing during much of their five- to eight-year life

81

Above: Steinbok avoid hilly country in favour of flat plains, often taking refuge underground.

Opposite: Gerenuk, the giraffe-necked gazelle of Kenya's desert lands.

Left: Kirk's dik-dik stands just over a foot high.

span, suni favour leaves, young shoots, roots, and a limited amount of grass. Almost independent of water, they are found locally throughout Kenya wherever there are forests. Their specific Latin name, *moschatus*, derives from the large gland below their eyes which gives off that strong musky odour.

Colourful in variety and contrasting in size, Kenya's family of duiker are an appealing group of shy and elusive antelope. Most common of all, the **Bush (or Grey) Duiker** stands around sixty-one centimetres from hoof to shoulder and weighs between eleven and thirteen kilos. Widespread throughout the country, there are many local variations in the size of the body, horns, colour and the thickness of the coat. In mountain regions this is unusually shaggy.

They are the only duiker found in open range and the most universal – ranging from sea level desert to snow line, although almost never in bamboo or dense forest. They are also the most adaptable of the duiker and have survived where others have become extinct. They are often found on farms – even in small vegetable gardens.

Forest Duikers are red in colour and move in a characteristically hunched posture, with their head close to the ground. It enables them to move more easily through thick and often tangled undergrowth, using their regular, well-marked trails and passages.

When alarmed, all duiker plunge into thick cover; hence their name, given them by the early Afrikaans settlers in Africa, from the Dutch word meaning 'Diver'.

6. Pigs, Hippos and Crocodiles

With its black tufted lance-like tail held vertically erect as it trots through the bush, the odd-looking **Wart Hog** is the most common of Kenya's wild pigs. Unmistakable with its greyish, naked skin covered with a few bristles on the back of its neck and shoulders, what gives the wart hog its real identity are the large wart-like growths and tusks on either side of its face.

When cornered or threatened, wart hogs are plucky and doughty fighters. Their tusks are formidable weapons. They are prolific in Kenya.

Usually gregarious – though old boars sometimes move round on their own – they form sounders of quite large numbers, often sleeping in adapted and enlarged old aardvark burrows, always entering in reverse, thus keeping their tusks to the forefront in the event of any attack. Mainly day creatures, they have poor sight but acute hearing and sense of smell. They kneel to graze on grass and herbs.

Game protection has encouraged the **Giant Forest Hog** to reveal itself more often. In the Aberdare National Park they can be seen easily. They are primarily grazers, but are only found in, and immediately about, the forests of Mount Kenya, Aberdares and the Mau.

The largest of the three Kenya pigs, they are heavily built – weighing between 100 to 200 kilos – and have a long, coarse coat and tufted tail.

Prominent swellings under the eyes give them a dissipated look. Males form small troops and sounders usually comprise of a master boar and from six to twelve hogs.

Below: Wart hog are doughty fighters when
threatened.

Below: Hippopotamus, distantly related to the pig family.

Their heavy upper tusks and razor-sharp lower tusks provide formidable defence when they are attacked.

The **Bush Pig** looks like a shaggy version of the domestic pig. These medium-size creatures – they weigh from fifty-four to eighty-two kilos – root voraciously for food, marking the area by tearing up the ground, overturning shrubs, and scattering debris over a wide area.

On the increase throughout Kenya because of protection, they now constitute a considerable hazard to peasant farmers. A sounder of bush pigs can do potent damage during a night's rooting on a small farm.

These basically nocturnal animals are omnivorous eaters – as well as roots and bulbs they gobble up reptiles, carrion, birds eggs, larvae, and insects.

They have sharp but short tusks and the older males have two prominent warts on their snouts. Bush pigs are found wherever there are thickets and forest, hiding in dense vegetation during the day. They are swift runners and strong swimmers when in flight.

Like Giant Forest Hog, the best places to see them are in the Mount Kenya and Aberdare forest parks.

The tusks of the **Hippopotamus** are contemptuously described as 'poor man's ivory'. This fat and heavy creature, which derives its name from the Greek word for 'River Horse', is more like a pig – to which it is distantly related – than an equine thoroughbred. It weighs up to four tonnes. Yet, immersed in water, the third-largest living land animal floats with unlikely grace along river or lake bed.

True amphibians, they can hold their breath and stay submerged for up to six minutes. They eat, mate, and give birth under the water. Their skin, a uniform brownish-grey, lightening to pink around the eyes, muzzle and throat, is frequently coloured red by a secretion from its sweat glands. Superstitious people in days of yore were convinced it was sweating blood, an idea no doubt encouraged by the beast's notorious temper and its capacity for murder and mayhem. Aroused, the hippo has been known to slice a man in half with one gash. The rule? Never come between a hippo and water.

These amphibians spend most of the day sleeping and resting, usually in the water, coming up frequently to blow air and recharge lungs. Around sundown the schools (or sounders) leave the water, adult bulls at the back, to spend the night within the limits of their 'home-range' – a pear-shaped area marked by well-defined pathways – in search of grass and other vegetation, amounting to around sixty kilos of fodder nightly for each animal.

Usually born in the water, the young are suckled at first on land. Hippo mothers are stern disciplinarians. Disobedient young are chastised, sometimes with a savage bite, and the youngster made to cower in submission. When a mother leaves the school to go off somewhere, other females take over as acting 'mothers'.

Living for around forty years in the wild, hippos are basically beneficial – stirring up the bottom layers to spread nutrients for fish to feed on and providing large and frequent amounts of fertilizer through their dung. They also keep weed and papyrus beds clear.

One hundred and sixty million years before the first of man's ancestors stood and walked upright along the shores of Lake Turkana in Kenya's north, the **Nile Crocodile** was proud and forbidding monarch of the lake's mudbanks and sandspits.

This most ancient of living creatures has barely changed from the time it was a diminutive cousin of the giant dinosaurs and long-extinct creatures of the misty, little-known epochs of prehistory.

Oddly, for all its sinister jawful of teeth, the crocodile is unable to chew. When it eats large prey, this reptile clamps down on its victim and threshes around in the water, often rotating several times, until the limb is wrenched from the trunk. To swallow, it raises its head and lets the food fall to the back of its throat. Digestion is slow. Bodies recovered from dead crocodiles fifteen hours after the reptile has made a kill have been virtually unmarked. Crocodiles kill with a blow of either the head or tail.

Cold-blooded, these saurians depend entirely on the external temperature to maintain their own – and regulate their body heat according to the time of day. They will leave the water early in the morning to warm up in the sun, returning to the water to escape the excessive heat of high noon, returning later in the now cooler day to bask in the sun once more until around sundown when they return to the water for the night.

Clutches of up to ninety eggs are laid about seventy to ninety centimetres beneath the lake or river bank. When ready to hatch, the young call their mother back to dig them out by grunting and chirruping inside their eggs. These tiddlers are easy prey for a host of hunters – from the monitor lizard through raptorial birds, to wild cats and mongooses.

Tenacious, crocodiles can remain submerged for periods of up to an hour. Nor do they relinquish life easily. One crocodile's heart, cut out from the corpse, continued to beat on its own for thirty minutes.

7. Hares and Rodents

Propped upright, resting on its powerful tail and squatting on its hind legs, the **Spring Hare** – not truly a hare at all – looks for all the world like a miniature kangaroo. All it lacks is the marsupial pouch in which to carry its young.

Although widespread throughout Kenya, it is rare to see one bounding through the bush, black tail bobbing up and down, for they are active only by night. They spend their day inside their burrows which normally have several entrances, all of them blocked from the inside. When they emerge at dusk they do so with one tremendous bound – leaping well clear and beyond their entrance – just in case any predator happens to be waiting in ambush. In one leap, they can clear a distance of more than eight metres.

Kenya's only true lagomorph, the **African Hare**, with its big ears, grizzled, black and buff body and long slender legs, is easily distinguishable. Widely distributed throughout Kenya, these solitary, nocturnal creatures with their large, typical hare-like eyes, much related to the European hare, are found in grassland, bush, and sparse woodland.

The number of squirrels in Kenya range from the friendly, inquisitive little ground squirrels, similar to their cousins in Europe and North America, to the unusual Flying Squirrel. Easily identified – they look like squirrels – there are more than a dozen species.

The **Striped Ground Squirrel** lives in burrows and has an almost naked belly. Found almost everywhere in Kenya's drier savannah, these delightful animals follow lodge visitors from room to dining area, scampering along, stopping to beg with quaint appeal, paws held together, whiskers twitching with touching pathos.

The **Unstriped Ground Squirrel** is the same size and has the same habits. Very sociable, it is a daytime creature, and lives in colonies – often with other species of rodents – excavating burrows which form warrens connected by tunnels spread over several square metres. They move with a peculiar jumping gait, tail arched behind.

Perhaps most fascinating of all is the rarely seen **Scaly-tailed Flying Squirrel**. Not really a squirrel at all, it belongs to a peculiar group of rodents, the *anomalares* – the only living remnants of a family now extinct outside Africa.

Spread out, its gliding membrane – a flap of furred skin from wrist to ankle down the body and from ankle to tail – forms a broad wind surface enabling the creature to 'plane' long distances. Beneath this membrane, near the tail, scales enable it to establish a firm grip on the tree on which it lands. In Kenya, it is found only in Kakamega and on Mount Elgon. It can 'fly' as far as ninety metres, though it normally only makes short flips – between fifteen to eighteen metres.

Below: Generally nocturnal, the African hare is
widely distributed throughout Kenya.

Opposite: African elephant, the world's largest
land creature.

8. Big Game and a Little One

Elephants need vast amounts of land on which to live, moving in their own timeless way from one pasturage to another, leaving the area behind to recover and rehabilitate itself. Today, boundaries, border posts, title deeds, and human settlement increasingly diminish the range of their territory. Migration trails are blocked and barred.

Yet, where they roam, the earth barely trembles with their footfalls. For all their size, these giants walk with the delicacy of a ballet dancer. In size or shape nothing looks farther removed from mankind than the elephant. Yet, in instinct and behaviour, the world's largest living land animal comes close to us in habit and organization and in its wilfulness to destroy the environment on which it depends.

Measuring almost four metres from hoof to shoulder, the **African Elephant** weighs anything from three-and-a-half to six-and-a-half tonnes and requires tremendous nourishment. They eat from ninety to 270 kilos of fodder a day and drink between 200 and 300 litres of water. To achieve this intake they depend almost entirely on the dexterity, flexibility, and strength of that astonishing appendage – an elongated nose – their trunk. They use this limb for scent and communication, for washing and cleaning, for carrying and clearing, and for drinking and eating. The tusks are simply secondary – but important – lifting, carrying, and clearing tools. These days male tusks seldom exceed forty-five kilos each, though the heaviest on record weighed 103 kilos and the longest, measured on the curve, was close to four metres. These upper incisors become visible on the young at about sixteen months and continue to grow through-out life.

In fact, an elephant's life span depends on its teeth, which are highly adapted to its mode of living. As one is worn away the one next to it moves down the jaw to push it out and replace it. When the last one has come forward and is worn down, at an age anywhere between fifty to seventy years, if from nothing else, the elephant must die of starvation.

The **Bush Elephant** walks with grace and ease, because the massive feet, made up of layers of elastic tissue, work rather like shoes with deep rubber soles. They average about six kilometres an hour when walking but, briefly, can reach forty kilometres an hour when charging – an astonishing speed considering their weight and size. There are noticeable differences between the African and Asian elephant: one is that the latter has only one 'lip' at the end of its trunk compared to the two 'lips' of the African. Nor do Asian females develop tusks.

It takes close to two years from conception to deliver the young, which weigh between 120 and 136 kilos. During labour the mother is attended by two other females – 'midwives' – who accompany her when she withdraws from the herd to give birth in discreet privacy.

Highly social, elephants move in herds that average between ten and twenty and sometimes exceed 1,000. Although their sight is poor, elephants have an excellent sense of smell and well-developed hearing, with a brain three times the weight of that of a human being – between 3.6 and five kilos. Elephants

Opposite: Elephant require up to forty gallons of water a day to survive.

Below: Two bull elephant joust for supremacy.

easily fell trees – as much as 1.2 to 1.5 metres thick – slowly pushing them over, forehead to trunk. In this way they swiftly transform woodlands into open grasslands.

In such a world of superior superlatives and diminishing diminutives it may come as a surprise to discover that the elephant's closest relative may be the pint-sized hyrax, cheeky-looking characters no bigger than rabbits.

There are two look-alike genera which measure about thirty centimetres from hoof-like paws to shoulders, and about 2.3 to four kilos in weight. In fact, superficially they look much like guinea-pigs. The nocturnal **Tree Hyrax** has remarkable soles, well adapted for climbing trees. They are kept continuously sticky by a substance released from a gland. Tree hyrax can be found at almost any altitude in almost any forest from sea level to around 4,000 metres.

Feeding throughout its ten years on an exclusively vegetarian diet of grass, berries, fruits, barks, lichens, and leaves, the beguiling, furry little tree hyrax is perhaps best known not as a relative of the elephant but for its scream. Delivered in the dead of night it sounds like the Devil incarnate. This intense, searing anguished cry in fact is a territorial call much like the lion's roar.

Lighter in colour, **Rock Hyrax** have feet which also enable them to move with astonishing agility in their chosen world of boulder and precipice. The sole has semi-elastic, rubber-like pads which provide a sure grip on all inclines in all conditions.

Daytime creatures, they live in large colonies and may be seen sunning themselves during the day on rocky hills or boulders in groups of between sixty and 100.

For such placid-looking creatures, about as active as an average farm cow or steer, the ferocity of the **African Buffalo** when roused is daunting. Not for nothing is this member of Africa's Big Five considered the most dangerous and ruthless of all wild animals – it is believed to have killed more hunters than any other. Incredibly strong and durable, this brave and ferocious beast is on the increase all over Kenya – benefitting not only from conservation and an undisturbed life within the reserves but also from the reduction and control of bovine diseases in domestic stock through the spread of veterinarian practices.

Buffaloes need plenty of fodder to maintain their strength and stamina. Although the West African forest version is considerably smaller, often almost half the weight, both races are voracious eaters, browsing and grazing on a variety of grasses, leaves, twigs, and young shoots for most of their fifteen to twenty years. Gregarious, they frequently form herds of 500 up to 2,000. Buffalo are found everywhere in Kenya, from sea level to mountain forests above the 3,000-metre contour, always close to water.

Measuring between two to three metres high from the tip of its two-toed claw to the crest of its bald head, the **Ostrich** is not the ridiculous bird that myth or legend make it out to be. Indeed, few creatures have adapted so well to their environment and its attendant dangers.

The largest living birds cannot fly. But they are endowed with a phenomenal turn of speed – up to sixty kilometres an hour in strides of four metres – enough to leave all but the swiftest of

Above: Baby elephant require constant contact and affection if they are to thrive.

Opposite: Elephant herd in Amboseli, Kilimanjaro in background.

Right: Rock hyrax, a distant and tiny relative of the elephant.

hunters behind. They can maintain fifty kilometres an hour for up to thirty minutes. On the run, however, they will often vanish abruptly from view. This sleight-of-feather is cunning deception. The ostriches stop in full stride and drop suddenly into a squatting position, extending their necks along the ground, a practice which gave rise to the legend that they bury their head in the sand.

In full stride they can bound up to a height of 1.5 metres and their lethal kick can bend an iron bar at right angles. They share the distinction of being a flightless, running bird with the look-alike rhea of South America, and the emu and cassawaries of the antipodes. Millions of years ago there were nine species of ostrich, but now only the African ostrich survives, characterized by its height, half of which is made up of its neck, and its two-toed foot, legs, and thighs.

Females are shabby brown with pale edgings to their feathers, the males much more dandy with vivid black and white plumes on the wings and tail. The mating ritual is boisterous and colourful. Females utter a deep booming call and the males – real randy-dandies – roar like lion, swell their necks like balloons, and chase around in groups, each trying to outshine the other, holding out their wings to show off their white plumes. The prize for the successful male is a harem of three to five hens. In this elaborate courtship, the cock and hen feed together, actually synchronizing the rhythm of the pecking movements of the head and neck. If the harmony is right, the male sits down and twists his neck as the hen walks round him in circles, eventually succumbing and dropping into a mating position. Eggs average fifteen to sixteen centimetres long and weigh up to 1.4 kilos.

An ostrich egg is as thick as a china cup and needs to be cracked open with a tough saw or hammer. One egg is equal to two or three dozen domestic eggs and tastes the same. Kept in a refrigerator, they remain fresh for up to a year. They take two hours to hard-boil. Eggs hatch after about six weeks incubation. Chicks can run almost as soon as they hatch. After only a month – they grow like weeds, six to eight centimetres a week – they can reach a speed of fifty-six kilometres an hour.

Ostrich have tough gullets and voracious appetites and have been known to swallow iron objects – coins, nails, horseshoes. Reared from the young, they make faithful pets.

The last ostrich in Saudi Arabia was shot in 1933 and the last one in Asia was seen in 1941. They flourish in the wild today in South Australia where they were introduced, and are bred in captivity in South Africa for the ostrich feather trade.

A series of special valves in the neck help the **Giraffe** to keep its blood pressure – and its balance – level when it moves its lofty head quickly. Nature has given the world's tallest creature several systems to help it cope with life as the 'skyscraper of the bush'. This includes a forty-five-centimetre-long tongue and a prehensile upper lip. Both help to rip away the leaves, shoots, and twigs of thorn trees without harm. A giraffe's tongue is the longest in the world. Only that of the pangolin comes close.

Measuring anything from 4.6 to 5.5 metres from the tip of its toe to the top of its head, the average giraffe weighs up to 1,272 kilos. Already more than 1.5 metres high at birth and around sixty-eight kilos in weight, the young continue to grow for the

first seven to ten of their twenty-five years. Both male and female are born with a variable number of short bony 'horns' on their head, sometimes with a knob on the centre of the forehead.

There are two races of the common giraffe in Kenya. The **Maasai Giraffe** is found mainly to the south-west of Athi River. The **Rothschild** is now found only in Lake Nakuru National Park.

The much less common **Reticulated Giraffe**, quite distinct, is undoubtedly the most handsome of Kenya's giraffe with its liver-red body covered with a network of delicate white lines – very different from the jagged blotches and rondels of the others. It is found north of the Tana River. There is also a hybrid race which roams the drylands between the Tana River and the Athi.

The enormous giraffe seems somehow shy and delicate, so much so that the first one received at the Imperial court in 15th-century Peking, a gift from the Sultan of Malindi, was considered the epitome of gentleness and peace.

Running in a curious and fascinating loping gallop, its sinuous gait results in speeds up to fifty-six kilometres. But not for long. A giraffe's lungs are inadequate. A short sprint leaves it panting and exhausted, in a state of collapse. These fitful moments of action would have even more dire consequences were it not for the complicated system of valves, reservoirs, and canals which keep the blood pumping along its 2.1-metre-long neck to the head. So successful are these that the change in blood pressure in the brain is monitored by the instant; in the fraction of a second between the rise and fall of the head which occurs with each stride the animal takes, and kept constant. Giraffe are more closely related to the deer family than any other living creature.

The **Zebra's** vivid and eye-catching stripes are unique among nature's handiwork. Of many millions which roam Africa, no two are alike. Just as a fingerprint distinguishes one human from another, so the zebra's stripes mark each creature as a wholly distinct individual.

Of the two species, the **Grevy's** is considered the more beautiful. Larger, heavier and taller than the **Common (or Burchell's)** Zebra, its stripes are much more numerous and narrower, black or dark brown, on a white cream background. The latter is smaller, more like a pony, with fewer and broader stripes, especially on the rump and hindquarters.

Zebra stallions fight ferociously for mates and dominance. These clashes are spectacular affairs with the rival stallions rearing and plunging, lashing out with both hind and forelegs, and neck wrestling. Occasionally, they will suddenly go down on their forelegs and slash savagely at each other's neck with bared teeth. They are generally dependent on water, needing to drink daily. Their smell, sight, and hearing are acute and they can sustain high speeds over short distances.

One unfortunate relative of the zebra was the **Quagga**, a South African species exterminated in 1861 – a fact only discovered when a zoo requested some replacements. To everybody's astonishment it was discovered that the quagga had been wiped out by hunters.

Thriving for more than sixty million years before the arrival of

Opposite: Reticulated giraffe. Special valves in the neck control the blood pressure of the world's tallest creature to compensate for sudden movement.

Below: African ostrich. Though the world's largest bird, it cannot fly.

mankind, the **Rhinoceros** has come close to extinction in Kenya in the last twenty years.

From a repository of around 20,000 at the start of the 1970s, the survivors in Kenya eighteen years later numbered fewer than 500. The tragic irony is that the horn on its nose for which it has been so indiscriminately slaughtered contains nothing more valuable than the keratin which makes up mankind's own fingernails.

Neither black nor white – the difference is one of semantics, not colouring – the **Black Rhinoceros** is the smaller of Kenya's two species, weighing around 907 to 1,364 kilos. The average size of its horns varies between fifty to eighty-nine centimetres for the front horn and just under fifty-three centimetres for the rear horn. Ironically, if the horns were removed when the animal was drugged, they would eventually grow back again. In one animal's lifetime it could perhaps yield triple the number of that single horn for which the poacher so ruthlessly takes its life.

With its relatively small feet, three toes on each hoof, and pointed prehensile upper lip, the black rhinoceros is a browser that used to be found anywhere from sea level up to 3,500-metre contour, from savannah to montane forest.

In a number of smaller reserves in Kenya where wardens can keep a closer guard over its movements it maintains a precarious hold on life. With a life span between thirty and forty years, the total stock of black rhinoceros in the whole world is now considered no more than 30,000.

Even fewer of the **White Rhinoceros**, which derives its name from the Afrikaans language of South Africa, *weit*, meaning wide-mouthed, remain. With its square lips this species is a grazer, not a browser – even more sedentary than its kin and much more docile and gregarious, moving in friendly families and groups of two to five.

Only two groups, imported, exist in Kenya. Found in Meru National Park and the private Solio Ranch, they are guarded night and day by game wardens who even herd them to their pastures each day. Nonetheless, in one swift surprise raid, setting off a bush fire as a diversion, poachers in the early 1980s managed to reduce the Meru numbers.

The white rhinoceros is a much more solid beast than the black and is normally a good fifteen centimetres higher at the shoulder and 2,032 to 4,064 kilos heavier, making it the biggest of all land animals after the elephant.

As Kenya's – and Africa's – human population grows at an unprecedented rate of four per cent a year, time and space has begun to run out – not only for the rhinoceros but for most wildlife.

Yet the conservative rhinoceros has made less demands on its habitat in sixty-four million years than mankind in three million. And while man boasts of his superior intelligence, it seems odd that we should accord ourselves a priority in terms of space and population that, clearly, is undeserved – especially when the *Beautiful Animals of Kenya* have shown us how to live as one with Planet Earth.

Opposite top: Grevy's zebra. Like fingerprints, no two zebra's stripes are ever identical.

Above: White rhinoceros.

Right: Black rhinoceros, smaller but less placid than the white.

Opposite: Burchell's zebra, distinguished from Grevy's by the different pattern of its stripes.

Index (Illustrations indicated by boldface numbers.)

Below: Black rhinoceros, Africa's most endangered species, is on the brink of extinction.

Overleaf and following pages: Elephant at water. Wildebeest and zebra struggle across the Mara River in their annual migration. Wildebeest at sunset. Giraffe at day's end on the African plain.